BEING MORE
THAN HUMAN

POCKET EDITION

Published from
Mardukite Borsippa HQ, San Luis Valley, Colorado
Mardukite Academy & Systemology Society
for spiritual or educational purposes only

BEING MORE THAN HUMAN

REDISCOVERING THE SPIRITUAL SELF

A Basic Course developed
by Joshua Free
for the Systemology Society

THE JOSHUA FREE IMPRINT
JFI PUBLICATIONS

© 2023, JOSHUA FREE

ISBN : 978-1-961509-18-4

Also available in hardcover as
"Fundamentals of Systemology"

Pocket Paperback Edition — *October 2023*

mardukite.com

SYSTEMOLOGY is the
"New Thought" of the 21st Century.

It is the study of how
Spiritual Beings with unlimited power
became entrapped in the
Human Condition.

This study is an applied philosophy
— "A Pathway to Ascension" —
that charts our way back out,
freeing the True Self to experience
higher levels of existence again.

Systemology is the true science of the
"Matrix."

After more than a decade of
development, the "Fundamentals of
Systemology" are concisely explored
here in the first official
"Basic Course" on the subject ever
given by Joshua Free for the
Mardukite Academy.

It's time to discover
who you really are...
because you
were never "Human."

Fundamentals of Systemology
Basic Course Lesson Booklets

Lesson #1
BEING MORE THAN HUMAN
Rediscovering the Spiritual Self

Lesson #2
REALITIES IN AGREEMENT
Spiritual Life and The Universe

Lesson #3
WINDOWS TO EXPERIENCE
The Filters of Human Perception

Lesson #4
ANCIENT SYSTEMOLOGY
Wisdom From the Arcane Tablets

Lesson #5
A HISTORY OF SYSTEMOLOGY
Evolution of a Spiritual Science

Lesson #6
SYSTEMOLOGY PROCESSING
Practices of Spiritual Awakening

TABLET OF CONTENTS

"BASIC COURSE" INTRODUCTION

LESSON ONE:
BEING MORE THAN HUMAN—
REDISCOVERING THE SPIRITUAL SELF

APPENDIX

INTRODUCTION
TO THE
"BASIC COURSE"

WELCOME, SEEKER!
YOUR JOURNEY ON THE PATHWAY
BEGINS HERE

This is a basic course in *Systemology* — specifically, the fundamental principles of *Mardukite Systemology*.

Quite simply: *Mardukite Systemology* is a new evolution in Human understanding about the "systems" governing *Spiritual Life*, *Reality*, the *Universe* and all *Existences*.

In many ways, *Systemology* is a 21st Century breakthrough that continues the legacy — and unifies the original pursuits — of early 20th Century *"American New Thought"* and other metaphysical schools of philosophy and mysticism. These are mostly all generalized (and often dismissed) in modern culture as *"New Age"* beliefs, though they are actually quite "*old*"—some even based on the most ancient known writings of discovered civilizations.

Mardukite Systemology was once concisely described as "an applied spiritual technology of the 21st Century A.D., based on spiritual wisdom from the 21st Century B.C." because of our use of "*Mesopotamian*" *Arcane Tablets* as source material for its foundations (and from which it retains a "*Mardukite*" designation).

The original *New Thought Movement* in America applied a "Western Civilization" approach to "Eastern" concepts—concepts that we now take for granted today, but of which were relatively unknown to the general population at that time. The movement sought to develop an "applied spiritual philosophy" whereby an individual could unlock their hidden potentials, untapped "*Knowingness*" and higher spiritual states of *Beingness*. These innate or native conditions of *Self* (as a *Spirit*) are blocked—or "fragmented"—by a "human" preoccupation with identifying *Self* as one and the same with the material body that it is merely using as a "vehicle" to experience (communicate and interact) within *this* Physical Universe.

Early *New Thought* work primarily emphasized practical "healing" applications (*mental healing, faith healing, &tc.*)—but at its very core, we may restate the ultimate pursuit or original focus was to "free humans *to be* their ideal native spiritual state."

This goal has been with us—lingering on the periphery of the "surface world"—for much longer than the existence of a *New Thought Movement*. In fact, for as long as "spiritual beings" have found themselves entrapped by a "Human Condition" and enforced to experience *this* "material existence" (fragmented from their true *Self*), a continuing pursuit has ensued to correct the situation—at least by those individuals still retaining enough *Awareness* to realize it.

Humans have been figuring on how to break free from the *"Matrix"* for a very long time. The desire or ambition to rise above the "standard-issue" Human Condition is already there. But the truth is that many other remotely similar "evolutions" of *New Thought* have dissolved into "multi-level marketing" schemes, "motivational pop-psychology" coaching, abusive "cult-like" movements—or heavily promoted books that skyrocket to the peaks of literary "bestseller lists" only to be discarded soon after and forgotten. They all share one thing in common: they all seem to capitalize on an innate desire or yearning we have to *"ascend"*—but, of course, without delivering stable results.

Even the most pious and well-meaning

philosophies and spiritual sciences have each fallen short of piercing the *"invisible barriers"* of perception separating *this* "Physical Universe" from any other "higher" existence—and with it, blocking our "way out" and the *Awareness* of our own true native state as an *Eternal Spirit*.

SYSTEMOLOGY:
21ST CENTURY NEW THOUGHT

Our *Systemology* is a new approach to *"Self-Actualization"*—completely relevant for the modern age and the future—and quite different from previous attempts or other traditions you might find.

Former attempts at overcoming *"barriers"* or *"gates"* of *reality* have included simply pretending that they don't exist, rejecting all material existence—all *time* and *space*—as an *"illusion"* and consequently losing the ability to actually *confront* the *reality* of anything *"As-It-Is."*

Our *Systemology* is also the answer to the "great mysteries" pervading the material sciences and natural philosophies; for they only seek to further qualify and validate the *reality agreements* made for *this* Physical Universe—and thus their level of understanding can never successfully pass the "barriers" either.

When applying our philosophy and techniques, the "systematic routes" outlined for an individual to increase their *"Actualized Awareness"* (and reach gradually higher toward their *"Spiritual Ascension"*) is referred to as *"The Pathway"*—and we call that individual a *"Seeker."*

At the start of *The Pathway*, early *routes* emphasize establishing a strong personal foundation of emotional well-being and mental strength before a *Seeker* is introduced to more advanced exercises and practices.

As a *Seeker* increases their *Awareness* in this lifetime, their spiritual "*Knowingness*" also increases—which is to say their sense of "*certainty*"; a certainty on *Life*, on this and other *Universes*, but more accurately, an increased certainty on *Self* as a practically unlimited "spiritual being" *having* an enforced restrictive "human experience."

One of the goals of "*Systematic Processing*" techniques in *Systemology* is to increase the ability of a *Seeker* to actually control and direct the "*attention*" of *Self* as a "spiritual being"—and as a result, *knowingly* increase command of the "human experience." This is a part of what we mean by "*Actualized Awareness*."

THREE STATES OF KNOWINGNESS

Raising a *Seeker's* level of *Actualized Awareness* requires, by definition, "bringing what is *hidden* (or not consciously known) up into the realm of *light* or *Knowingness*." We might go as far to say, as an imperfect example, that there are three primary states of *Knowingness*: *actual knowing*, *almost knowing* and *not-knowing*.

Actual knowing is what an individual is conscious of and can easily recall as needed. It makes up our "surface" (or "above-the-surface") thoughts; what is *"actually known"* and available to *Self* for "inspection" or analytical thought. This includes what we have *certainty* on as part of our *reality*.

Then, there are other *things* "below-the-

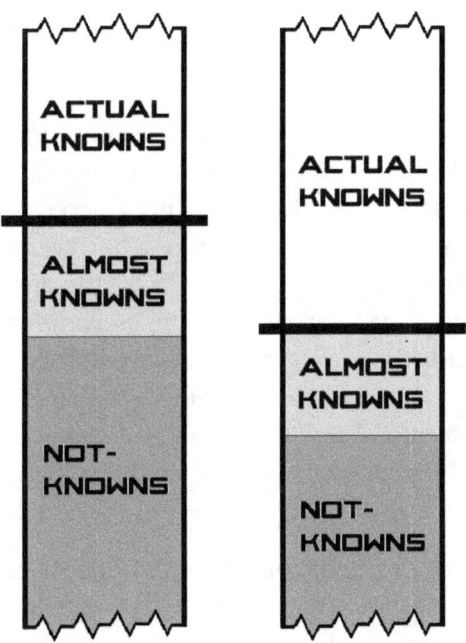

surface" that we do not easily remember (or have any *reality* on)—and these fit our other categories of *almost knowing* and *not-knowing*. The difference between these other two states is how *far* "below-the-surface" a *thing* is.

What you *"almost know"* are those *things* just "below-the-surface"—so *close* to the "surface" that they are almost accessible. This "gray area" includes what an individual is *uncertain* of. With a little assistance (*"Systematic Processing"* techniques), you can actually move a *thing* that is *"almost known"* to an "above-the-surface" state of *"actually knowing"* or remembering again. Only then may it be treated with any *certainty*.

There are also memories very deeply buried "below-the-surface." This includes suppressed data that is not currently accessible—and therefore, presently *"not-known."* Once again, there is a way to move *things* from this state into another state. For this to happen, the previous *"almost known" things* ("just-below-the-surface") need to be "purged" (at least partially) by *"resurfacing"* them into *"actually known" things*.

As more layers of *"almost knowns"* are *resurfaced* into *"actual knowns,"* more of what is *"not-known"* becomes accessible within the "gray area." *Systematic Processing* techniques of *Systemology* are intended to target this "gray area"—promoting increased *realizations* by elevating more knowledge to a state of *Actual Awareness*.

HOW TO STUDY
A SYSTEMOLOGY COURSE

Most *Seekers* study and practice *Systemology* at-a-distance and independent of the

"Mardukite Academy" or any "Master-level" mentors trained therein. This means that the *books* (and to a lesser degree, the *internet*) are the only means of direct contact a *Seeker* maintains with the "Systemology Society" during their studies.

It is quite common to have had negative past experiences with "education" and "learning"—whether in school or other type of instruction. This can sometimes inhibit an individual from pursuing a new *study* later on in their lifetime. However, simply following a few guidelines, ensures a *Seeker's* successful and positive experience when studying this course book—and, of course, the subject of *Systemology* as a whole.

To effectively study and understand a new subject (or a higher gradient of a subject), an individual must be "interested" in the material. A *Seeker* chooses to study *Systemology* because they "want" to, which is to say, on their own "*Self-Determinism*." While modern society likes to enforce "agreement" (to further solidify a *reality*), a genuine "interest" and true "understanding" can only occur on one's own *Self-Determinism*.

Having established interest, the next *barrier* to understanding is "vocabulary" (words) and "semantics" (meaning). Any specific study, science or tradition is distinguished by the *words* used to communicate it. For true communication to occur, the intended "meaning" for each "word" used must be clearly defined and perfectly understood by the reader or receiver. We call this "*A-for-A*" or "*one-to-one*" communication.

Misunderstood words are the most common reason an individual abandons studying a subject. To relay a proper communication of *Systemology* concepts to a *Seeker*, we use very specific language in our course books. There are newer concepts that more obviously require defining when introduced; and some of our terminology uses familiar words, but with a different or specific meaning than when used elsewhere.

When a misunderstanding occurs, *Awareness* declines. These generally begin to "stack up" after the first occurrence and the level of interest and attention will also decline. This is how a "confusion" develops and the individual will get "bored" with the subject, feel tired, and unable to concentrate.

In extreme cases of confusion, there will be no future interest in studying or "looking at" something further. Feelings of "anger" and "sadness" may result (because one had originally *intended* on knowing something), followed by lower-level opposing "considerations" such as:

"didn't really want to know" or "it probably isn't very good anyways."

The misunderstood word that an individual passed in their study may not be immediately obvious. One solution is to return to the part of the material that was still interesting and enjoyable to read. When scanning around that area of text, there is likely to be a new word (or specific use of a familiar word) that is unclear, but was passed by unnoticed. All *Systemology* books include their own *glossary*. Using this *glossary* and a high-quality dictionary will help resolve this misunderstanding once it is located.

With "interest" and "understanding" secure, the next challenge of learning concerns making a subject *"tangible"* —which means handling it as a "some-*thing*" in the individual's personal *reality* or *Universe*.

Studying intellectual or "philosophical" subjects from a *book* requires excessive amounts of *"thought creation"*—of handling many conceptual images and ideas *"imagined"* solidly in one's "mind" in order to actually "look at" what one is studying. These also require a certain amount of present-time *attention* or *Awareness* to sustain a continual *creation*.

When an individual lacks "objective" examples (objects, graphic representations or direct experience) to examine, they may become "overwhelmed" by "mental-mass" if maintaining too many of their own *images*. This prompts feelings of being "worn out" or "weighed down"—and *considerations* that one "must take a break" or that the subject is "too difficult."

The obvious remedy is to supplement "book-learning" with objective or physical examples. Rather than simply studying or memorizing a series of "dry facts" from an "outside source" (and then returning to "ordinary" life), a student that does understand the material will take it up as their "own" *viewpoint*.

By taking the philosophies up as one's "own" *viewpoint*, the materially is effectively "owned" by the individual. They are not *looking* through a *lens* of someone else. The *"responsibility"* taken by this *ownership* means the freedom to apply information to everyday life and determine the truth of a matter for one's *Self*.

The final *barrier* to learning is the *knowledge* (or "know-*ledge*") itself—the *ledge* or *level* from which a person *knows* or *understands*. A "basic fact" could have many *levels* of potential understanding. To interpret *reality*, an individual "stands" on the *ledge-level* (or *gradient*) of *Knowingness* they have the most "certainty" on.

An effective education of any subject is

27

taught on a *gradient*. This is what is intended by introducing the study of something in "*grades*." Rather than treating a subject as one total mass, true learning is achieved by increasing one's understanding on a *gradual* incline upward. The *ascent* to a mountaintop is not successfully achieved in one leap, but by targeting and reaching specific checkpoints along the way.

In 2019, the "*Grades*" were established for the "Mardukite Academy" to properly indicate what level of understanding a specific book or course is intended for. The entry-point to directly study materials of the Systemology Society at the Academy is "*Grade-III*." Lower *grades* pertain to other *Mardukite* subjects treated separately from Systemology. Higher *grades* continue to explore the "theories and practices" of the Systemology Society as a complete "*Pathway to Ascension*."

This *Basic Course* consists of a series of lessons (booklets) that teach the *"Fundamentals of Systemology."* It is an appropriate entry-point for a new *Systemology* student. It is also applicable to more advanced *Seekers* wanting to increase their *certainty* of understanding at higher *grades* as well.

To study *Systemology* just like a student at the Academy: a *Seeker* reads through all instructional material in a *Basic Course* lesson (booklet) and then performs any practical exercises indicated at the end. Before continuing on to the next lesson (booklet), the material is read again and the light exercises are reapplied.

The second pass through the material is likely to result in different *"realizations"* (an increased *level of understanding*) than the first time. Exercises may seem more vivid or significant. *Seekers* should feel cheerful and confident in their *understan-*

ding of a section (or lesson) before proceeding even further on *The Pathway*.

YOUR FIRST STEPS ON THE PATHWAY

Systemology is a "holistic" approach to understanding the human experience. It is not actually a singular "subject" in itself, but rather, a way to "view" the many "subjects" of *Life* and all *Existence*. Its "scope" is not restricted to the rigidly fixed *considerations* of any one "subject" exclusively. Yet, for us to properly communicate its specific intended meaning, *Systemology* does require its own unique basic vocabulary.

The "basic vocabulary" and "*Fundamentals*" of *Systemology* are studied together early on *The Pathway*. They are consistent for the remaining upper-*grades*. It is our *understanding* of them that evolves as we progress.

The entire structure of *Systemology* rests on foundations of earlier material and earlier researches—such as those found in the earlier *grades* of Mardukite Academy. However, in 2019, new developments made it possible for a *Seeker* to start upon *The Pathway* without first spending years navigating around the pitfalls of other avenues and earlier *grade* subjects. As an extension of the original Academy, the Systemology Society continues to map and define the upper-*grade routes* of our philosophy.

The *Fundamentals of Systemology* are explored throughout the *Basic Course*. The critical foundations of its vocabulary and concepts (from *Grade-II*) were concisely collected in 2019 as an essay—"*Mardukite Zuism: A Brief Introduction*." It is summarized below to provide a more complete introduction to the "lessons" of the *Basic Course*. Each "lesson" will go on to examine this data in greater detail.

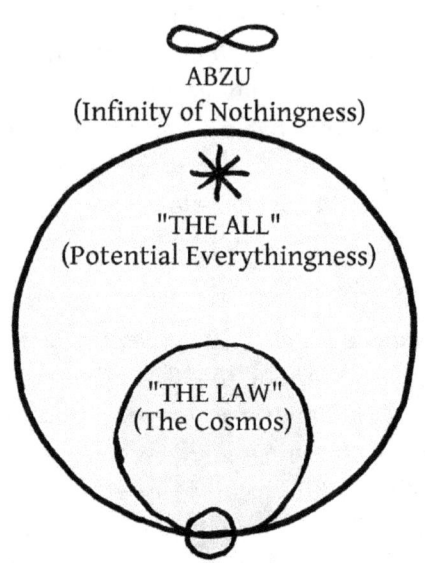

ABZU
(Infinity of Nothingness)

"THE ALL"
(Potential Everythingness)

"THE LAW"
(The Cosmos)

FOUNDATIONS OF SYSTEMOLOGY

Mardukite Zuism is a precursor to *Systemology*. It concerns an intensive archaeological study into the *Arcane Tablets* of Ancient Mesopotamia. Such tablet writings were once used to systematize an understanding of all cosmic knowledge— and they include the Babylonian *Epic of Creation*.

The *Epic of Creation* describes *ALL* ("ANKI") as separated into two *existences*: "AN" and "KI"—literally "heaven" and "earth"—which is to say *"spiritual"* ("AN") and *"physical"* ("KI"). Exterior to, and beyond, the *"potential everythingness"* of all *spiritual* existence and *physical* existence is only an Infinity of Nothingness ("ABZU").

In *Systemology*, we refer to the same two separate states of existence as *"Alpha"*

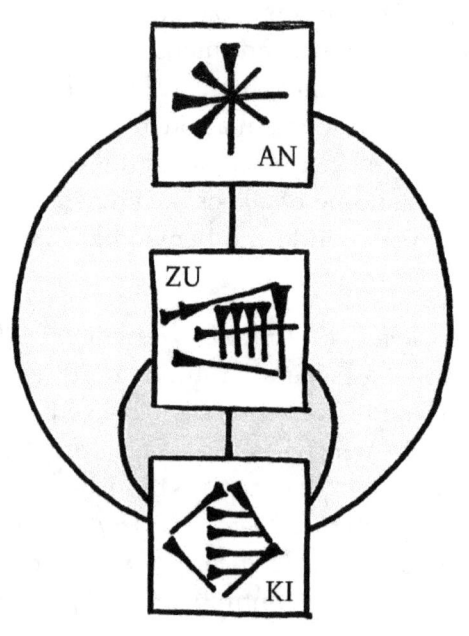

(*spiritual*) and "*Beta*" (*physical*). They are connected only by "*Spiritual Life Awareness*" or "ZU"—a term we have retained in *Systemology* (and for which *Mardukite Zuism* is named). Therefore, we have "*spiritual systems*" and "*physical systems*" connected by "ZU."

The "*Alpha*" *Universe*—of "metaphysical" or "spiritual" energy-matter—is not dependent on the "*Beta*" *Universe* to exist. The two exist independent of one another, except for a single channel or conduit maintaining a connection, which *is* the *Awareness* (the *Spiritual Life-Energy* or "ZU") of an "*Alpha-Spirit*."

"ZU" originates from an "*Alpha*" (*spiritual*) state, separate and distinct from the conditions of "*Beta*" existence that we experience as the *Physical Universe*. "ZU" is *Awareness*—the *Life-Force* or *Thought-Power* that "acts" or "impinges" on an "organism" in *Beta-Existence*.

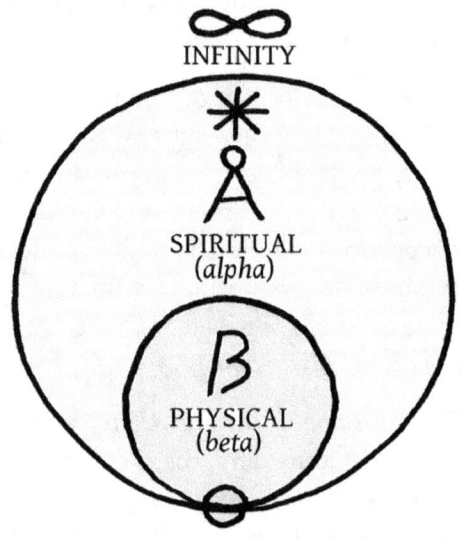

For example: the "intention" to read this book, or "commanding" a body to turn a page—those specific components are not actually a part of *this* existence. They are manifestations of a *Spiritual Awareness* (*Alpha*) acting upon an "organic body" (*Beta*). The *"Alpha-Spirit"* is the actual "Eternal" *Self*, which perceives and engages with *Beta-Existence* (*e.g.,* "Life on Earth") by using a "temporary" organic body or *"genetic vehicle."*

The *Alpha-Spirit* engages a *"ZU-Line"*—a *spiritual* "life-line" of *Attention* and *Awareness* ("ZU") energy—to an "organic body" or *genetic-vehicle* in order to directly experience a *"physical"* Beta-Existence.

We use the term *"Self-Honesty"* in *Systemology* to describe the original native *"Alpha"* state of true *Self-Directed* "Beingness" and crystal clear *"Knowingness." Self-Honesty* is the most basic "personality" or

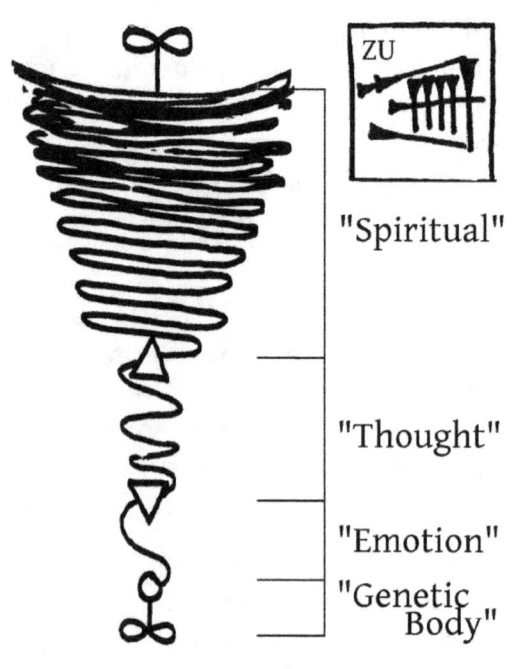

ZU

"Spiritual"

"Thought"

"Emotion"

"Genetic Body"

38

true expression of *Self* (*Alpha-Spirit*) as "*I-AM*"—a *Self-Determined* state that is *free* of artificial attachments, automatic reaction-response mechanisms, or enforced (*other-determined*) "*reality-agreements*" concerning the Human Condition.

Applying philosophic routes and systematic methods of *Systemology* in order to return *Awareness* of *Self* to its true "*Source*" is referred to as "*The Pathway*." Its structure is based on archaic "models" from the "Ancient Near East" (*Mesopotamia, &tc.*) and elsewhere—such as the "*Chakras*," the Babylonian "*Ladder of Lights*" (*Star-Gates*), and several versions of "*Kabbalah*."

For example: the Mesopotamians built "stepped-pyramids" as temples—called "*ziggurats*"—serving to remind us of the "ZU" bridging the *spiritual* and *physical* systems. Babylonians constructed *ziggurats* to correspond with *seven* primary "steps" or "*Gates*."

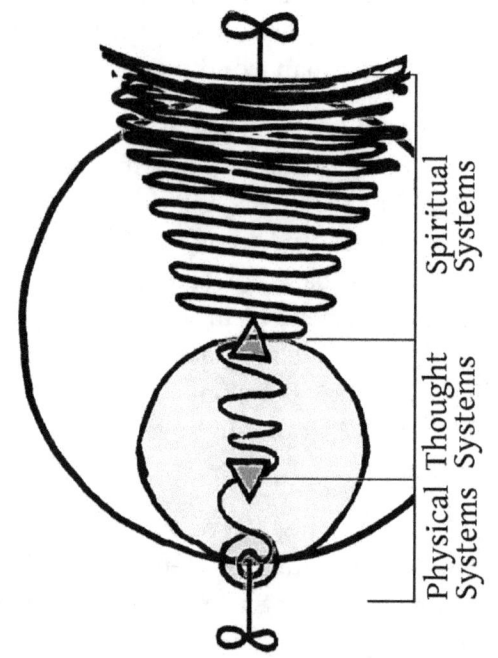

Spiritual Systems

Physical Thought
Systems Systems

40

The "gradients" or "tiers" of the Babylonian *Ladder of Lights* represent *The Pathway,* because they define the *levels* of *Actualized Awareness* (and *Self-Honesty*)—the states of *Self-purification*—between the "standard-issue" *Human Condition* and *Infinity.* This is the *route* we travel for our "*spiritual defragmentation*" or *Ascension.*

BASIC VOCABULARY REVIEW PUZZLE

ACROSS

3. The standard-issue default manner of filtering perceptions of the world on Earth, as Self is experiencing it. (*2 words*)

4. The condition of being misaligned, broken apart, shattered, fractured, distorted, or otherwise separated into parts, compared to its original state.

7. A student or practitioner studying and applying Systemology philosophy.

8. The True Self or I-AM Awareness. (*2 words, hyphenated*)

10. The nature of the Physical Universe or material existence.

11. Another way to say "the agreement about what something is."

DOWN

1. The physical body, or any organic life, may serve as your ___. (*2 words*)

2. Regimen or routine of Systemology practices, techniques or exercises that increase Actualized Awareness of Self.

5. Returning to the original native state (or Source of the Spiritual Self) is known universally as ____.

6. A stream of energy connecting Spiritual Awareness to physical existence. (*2 words, hyphenated*)

9. The progressive journey taken in Systemology is referred to as "*The* ___."

LESSON ONE:
REDISCOVERING
THE SPIRITUAL SELF

LESSON ONE
REDISCOVERING
THE SPIRITUAL SELF

The primary subject of our study in *Systemology* is YOU.

The most important component of all *Life* and *Existence* is the *Awareness*—the *Individual* themselves—that is observing and experiencing it. *Systemology* provides a "systematic" understanding of the parts (or "systems") that make up the *Individual* and the package of experience we call the *"Human Condition."*

A *Seeker* has likely heard of the *"Body, Mind and Spirit"* triad before—whether from "New Age" media or some other "holistic" practice. In spite of *cliché* references in culture, no attempt to effectively understand and command these interconnected systems has ever been fully completed prior to our *Systemology*.

Humans have spent countless lifetimes questing—*seeking*—for the *"Answer"* to the "great mystery" of *Life* and *Existence*; and ultimately our *Self*. Results of this search have become a massive *confusion*; so much so that many believe that these things are simply not to be known with any certainty. But these things *can* be known about in *this* lifetime.

Previous attempts to understand the connection between *"Body, Mind and Spirit"* have always occurred in *that* order of importance. But "material sciences" have never moved beyond observation of a *"body"*—of the *physical*—and are therefore incapable of perceiving *reality* at any "higher" level of understanding.

Even "psychology"—by definition, a study of the *"Mind and Spirit"*—quickly succumbed to evolve as a behavioral neuroscience about the "brain" when its originally defined purpose could not be reduced to a material science. In clinical practice today, it is little more than physiological and pharmaceutical medicine.

The *"Answer"* to *Life* and *Existence* is the *Spiritual Self.* The "mystery" is simply the *confusion.* There is no actual "mystery." However, as long as all attention is placed on trying to understand what's "out there" independent of the individual themselves, the *"Answer"* will not be understood because the right *"Question"* is not being asked.

Our subject is not about some "new" discovery or the domination of some "new" territory—and it doesn't require a "new" age in order to bring it about. It is about reclaiming what we have lost *Awareness* of; what has been *veiled*; what has been *concealed* from view—but it is still right there, because it is the *real* YOU.

The Answer is not found by accumulating more levels of *fragmentation* (as other "esoteric traditions" have done). *The Key* is a "sequential" and "systematic" removal of artificial layers—*reality-agreements* that have tracked behind us as we descended from once *knowingly* being a *God-like Awareness*, to now being confined within viewpoints of the *Human Condition*.

"*Rediscovering the Spiritual Self*" is not only the title of this first lesson; it is what defines our progressive journey all along the *Pathway to Ascension*—and, perhaps, is a perfect definition for the entire *Pathway* itself.

Every lesson, technique and exercise in *Systemology* is intended to increase an individual's "*Actualized Awareness*" a little more. The upper-level goal is for *Self* to perceive its own *Beingness* as a actual

"Spirit"—a viewpoint of an *Awareness* that exists separate from, and exterior to, *this* Universe. This is our true state. To be consistent in our philosophy, we refer to this native *"Alpha"* state of the individual as the *"Alpha-Spirit."*

The *"Alpha-Spirit" is* the individual; it is *you*; it is *me*; it is the "basic personality" of *Self* as a *Spiritual Being* underlying all of the fragmentation of our *Knowingness.* A continuous reduction of *Awareness* has kept us from accessing the virtually un-limited *Spiritual Power* we can *knowingly* command as an *Alpha-Spirit.*

Our *Spiritual Power* (or "ZU") is not actu-ally "lost" to us. It still trails behind us— but it *is* "entangled" in the continuous compulsive creation of our own frag-mentation *unknowingly.* Therefore, our *Spiritual Power*, our *Awareness*, and our handling of *Life* and *Existence*, are all in-terconnected.

51

By emphasizing our focus on identifying the *"Spirit"* or *Alpha-Spirit*—the actual *"I-AM" Awareness*—we immediately discover the original nature of the true *Self*. An individual is not a *"Mind"* or a *"Body,"* but a *Spiritual Awareness* with an ability to create and make use of these other "systems"—even if this is happening "automatically" and without *actually* being "aware" of it.

At our source, as an *Alpha-Spirit*, the fact that we continue to exist is not simply a result of our thinking it is so. *"Actualized Awareness"* is more than just: "I think, therefore I know." It is the actual *Awareness* of being *Aware*—being *Aware* of the "thinking" and the "knowing."

We do, however, have the ability to "lower" our "seat" of *Beingness* (and thereby block our *Knowingness*) so that we experience the "effects" of our *reality-agreements*. This means we have the power to descend from our *"All-Knowing"* state at will, and "cause" our *Self* to *"not-know"* things.

Of course, forgetting that we have done this does create some complications for us. In *Systemology*, we apply our philosophy to correct this—systematically retracing the routes taken by an individual to bring them to their present state. This is done on a *"gradient"* course—gradually and cumulatively handling what is most accessible at each step.

The *Alpha-Spirit* is not actually a "thing" located anywhere in the space-time of *this* Physical Universe (*Beta-Existence*). It does, however, have an ability to locate its own viewpoint by *reality-agreements*. It can change its "seat of consciousness" to relatively "remote" positions—including a *"Mind"* or *"Body."*

There is often a tendency to rigidly fix or "snap-in" one's attention—and "point-of-view" or "point-to-view-from"—on the "interior" of, for example, a *Mind-System*; or as in most cases on Earth, inside a "*genetic-vehicle*" (*Body*). This is what we really mean when we say that someone is "stuck in their head" or is "thinking with their (insert body part here)."

Here we begin to see details appear concerning "*Body, Mind and Spirit*" as separate, but interconnected, basic "systems" of the *Human Condition.* And an individual can also "*identify*" so greatly with a "thing" as to confuse its own *Beingness*— going so far as to believe itself to actually be purely *Human* above all else.

THE HUMAN CONDITION

An *Alpha-Spirit* can command a "*Body*"— or any "system"—directly by "reaching" with "energy-beams." But, as these impulses and intentions became more un-knowingly automated, they developed into an energetic-mass (a "mechanistic construct") that we call a "*Mind*."

This "*Mind*" is a communication system (relaying "ZU")—an intermediary used by an *Alpha-Spirit* to control a "*Body*."Of course, in the case of the standard-issue *Human Condition*, the *Alpha-Spirit* also be-lieves that they *are* that "*Body*"—when it is really only a *genetic-vehicle* used to per-ceive and act in *Beta-Existence*.

The Mind-System may be thought of as an "energy channel" or conduit between the *Awareness* of the *Alpha-Spirit* and the perceptions (and activities) of *Beta-Exist-ence*. The greater the "mass" composing the Mind-System, the less *Actualized Awareness* an individual is experiencing. This "mental-mass" adds "resistance" and "filters" to an otherwise free-flow of energy.

There is a primary part of the "Mind-System" that the *Alpha-Spirit* develops, compulsively creates, and then carries through its own existence. We call this the *"Master Control Center"* (or "MCC") in *Systemology*. Its function is mainly "analytical"—the part we use to "figure about" data and things we experience.

The *Master Control Center* ("MCC") allows the *Alpha-Spirit* to "evaluate" conditions by *differentiating* the data accumulated. Its contents is sorted by *"association"*—that "things" are related to other "things." It is how we "isolate" or distinguish different parts or *"facets"* of an encounter and determine their meaning.

There is also a part of the "Mind System" maintained at a mostly "cellular" level by the *genetic-vehicle*. We call this the *"Reactive Control Center"* (or "RCC") in *Systemology*, because it is primarily a network of

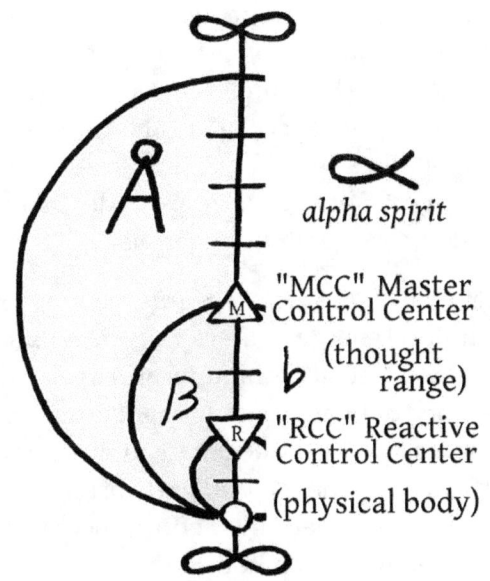

alpha spirit

"MCC" Master
Control Center

(thought
range)

"RCC" Reactive
Control Center

(physical body)

stimulus-response mechanisms designed to automatically preserve material "survival" of the organism.

The *Reactive Control Center* ("RCC") does not *differentiate* its data. Its contents is sorted by *"identification"* —that "things" are "things." Therefore, if a situation threatens the "survival" of the *genetic-vehicle*, all data from the encounter—any of its aspects or *"facets"* —are "identified" together as equally "dangerous."

Generally, the *Alpha-Spirit* no longer handles "energy" directly in *Beta-Existence*. The *"Mind"* communicates a relay of sensory data and environmental impressions from the *genetic-vehicle* to the *Alpha-Spirit*; and the *Alpha-Spirit* uses it to gauge or estimate the "effort" necessary for intended action in *Beta-Existence*.

Combined, the parts of the *"Mind"* (system) contribute to an *Alpha-Spirit's* experience of the *Human Condition*.

If *Awareness* of the *Alpha-Spirit* is "entangled" in *fragmentation* of mental-mass, then there is no clear communication of energy (or data); and therefore, a *"Self-Honest"* experience of *Life* is not possible.

The purpose of *Systemology* as an "applied philosophy" is to research and develop techniques that allow an individual to increase *Actualized Awareness* by *"defragmenting"* the Mind-System. It is not very concerned with the "anatomy" and "physiology" of *genetic-vehicles* directly. The parts of organic systems within *Beta-Existence* are already identified and defined by other "material sciences" and may be studied elsewhere.

BETA AWARENESS

The native state of the *Alpha-Spirit* is "exterior" to *this* Physical Universe and therefore its total capabilities of *Actualized Awareness* extend far beyond the *Human Condition*. When a fragmented "Mind-of-Spirit" (or MCC) and "Mind-of-Body" (or RCC) are combined, the potential range of experience is restricted.

In *Systemology*, the range of perception limited to *Beta-Existence* is referred to as "*Beta-Awareness*." This is what essentially defines the *Human Condition*; because it *is* a "condition" that affects the ideal operations of the *Alpha-Spirit* and other modes of thought and behavior that the individual believes they are originating.

Most individuals assume that they are totally *Self-Directed* and *Self-Determined* in their everyday *Life*—and that they are experiencing *Reality* with clarity. But *fragmentation* hinders this crystal clarity. *Beta-Awareness* is the *Actualized Awareness* (and level of *Self-Honesty*) one maintains in daily activities of a *Human* experience.

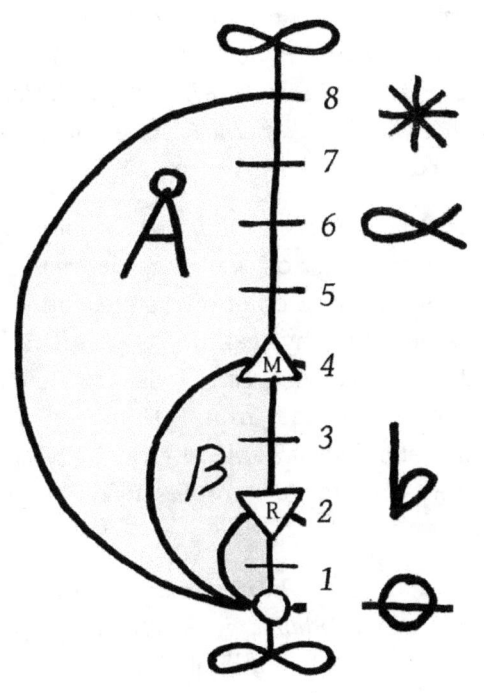

The gradients of perceptible *Beta-Aware-ness* "*interior*" to *Beta-Existence* and the *Human Condition* (*Alpha-Spirit* + *genetic-vehicle*) are treated in *Systemology* as the "*Beta-Awareness Scale.*" This scale directly relates to the "*Standard Model*" of *Systemology*. The *Standard Model* is explored in more detail later in "Lesson 2."

The *Beta-Awareness Scale* is a systematic understanding of varying degrees of thought activity, emotional states, and ultimately, the physical efforts of an individual. *Beta-Awareness* is relatively treated on a scale from "0" to "4." The complete *Standard Model* in *Systemology* extends up to "8" — representing "*Infinity.*"

We use the *Beta-Awareness Scale* portion of the *ZU-Line* (*Standard Model*) to "graph" or represent all gradient degrees of *Human* perception between two states: a fully expressed total *Self-Actualized Beta-*

Awareness (at "4.0") and organic death of the physical body or *genetic-vehicle* (at "0.0").

Both main parts of the Mind-System are also depicted on the *Beta-Awareness Scale*. The *Master Control Center* (MCC) is the point of "contact" between *Alpha* (above "4") and the *Human Condition* (below "4"). Therefore we place the MCC at "4"—and the range of *"Beta-Thought" fragmentation* between "2.1" and "4."

The *Reactive Control Center* (RCC) is plotted at "2." It governs the lower gradients of *Beta-Awareness*, which includes many "reaction-response mechanisms" inherent to the development, evolution and survival of organic-physical *Life*. The standard emotional range of the *Human Condition* is between "0.1" and "2."

THE BETA-AWARENESS SCALE

4.0 SELF-HONESTY (BETA)

3.9 "Vibrant" ("Charismatic")

3.8 "Enthusiastic" ("In Love")

3.7 "Energetic"

3.6 "Cheerful"

3.5 CONFIDENT ("Positive")

3.4 "Determined"

3.3 "Eager"

3.2 "Alert" ("Attentive")

3.1 "Strong Interest"

3.0 INTERESTED ("Content")

2.9 "Small Interest"

2.8 "Encouraged"

2.7 "Disinterested"

2.6 "Doubtful"

2.5 INDIFFERENT ("Tolerant")

2.4 "Bored"

2.3 "Dislike" ("Neglectful")

2.2 "Tired"

2.1 "Monotony"

2.0   INVALIDATING ("Pessimistic")
1.9   "Antagonism"
1.8   "Suffering" ("In Pain")
1.7   "Confrontational"
1.6   "Violent"
1.5   ANGRY ("Negative")
1.4   "Hateful"
1.3   "Spiteful"
1.2   "Resentment"
1.1   "Anxiety"
1.0   FEAR ("Afraid")
0.9   "Terror"
0.8   "Numb"
0.7   "Evasive"
0.6   "Loss"
0.5   GRIEF ("Sadness")
0.4   "Depression"
0.3   "Victimization"
0.2   "Hopelessness"
0.1   "Apathy" ("Unconsciousness")
0.0   BETA CONTINUITY (Organic Death)

It is important for us to mention that what is implied by *"emotional"* is really a reference to "negative" states of the *Human Condition*—which are all "reactionary" in nature—such as hopelessness, fear, anger, even pain. We treat enthusiasm, interest, boredom, and such, as "states of mind" or *thought* (above "2").

UNDERSTANDING BETA-AWARENESS

The *Beta-Awareness Scale* portion of the *Standard Model* of *Systemology* shares many similarities with the traditional idea of a "Pyramid of Self-Actualization" (originally proposed by the psychologist, Abraham Maslow). Both models demonstrate a systematic pattern of *Human* "in-the-body" experience and behavior.

As a *Seeker* increases their familiarity with the *"Fundamentals of Systemology,"* they discover more about themselves as an *Alpha-Spirit*—and others sharing the *Human Condition*. This type of knowledge leads to "true understanding" that should predict future results or behaviors when properly "evaluated."

Lower levels of *Awareness* relate to states of "emotional turbulence" *encoded* by experiences that are of a "destructive" nature and lead one to reject *Beta-Existence*, often with *force*. Higher levels promote a greater motivation toward achievement and an increased ability to confront and/or change existence *"As-It-Is."*

Obviously, if an individual is experiencing emotional turbulence, they are not "thinking clearly." They are operating from a point-of-view (or "seat of consciousness") that is *beneath* the level of thought and reason.

Between "0" and "4" are various degrees

of "*Beta-Fragmentation*" that affect clear perception for the *Alpha-Spirit* when participating with *Beta-Existence*. As an individual becomes more the "effect" of *Beta-Existence*, their level of *Awareness* lowers. An *Alpha-Spirit's* ideal position for involvement in *Life* is at "cause."

Beta-Awareness is not only affected by conditions present in one's environment. It is also affected by the *fragmentation* from past-experiences; the "stimulation" (or *resurfacing*) of past impressions (or "*imprints*") that are entangled with specific aspects (or "*facets*") of a situation— and then treated as if they *are* present.

This *fragmentation* affects the clear *Self-Honest* handling of *Reality* by adding false information about present-time conditions. Artificial data is "superimposed" on top of what one is experiencing and agreed to as *Reality*. As a result, the level of *Awareness* lowers, and the individual has more difficulties managing *Life*.

At lower *Awareness* levels, an individual is mainly only seeking and acting in their environment to meet the most basic demands of material survival. Only once these "needs" are met does the idea of greater stability enter in; and with stability established, eventually extending a further "reach" into groups or society—and toward achievement of relative success. This is what the "Pyramid of Self-Actualization" *tiers* demonstrate.

Certainly, *Awareness* levels will fluctuate based on innumerable factors. But, there is also a continuous or chronic state that is maintained in the absence of fluctuation—the "default" position that an individual is likely to operate from most of the time. [This may even differ from the *mask* they try to maintain socially.]

For example: When impressions of past-experience prompt a realization that *loss* is possible, an individual experiences *anxiety* ("1.1"), but *fear* ("1.0") sets in if sensing *loss* is inevitable, and then *terror* ("0.9") once it is about to take place. After experiencing *loss* ("0.6"), if unattended, they succumb to *grief* ("0.5"), and so on.

A *Systemologist* learns to observe the basic patterns of the *Human Condition* so that they do not fall prey to the automatic nature of it. We all experience "ups" and "downs" in the *game* of *Life*—but how "low" we go and how long we remain there indicates just how *Actualized* we have become again as an *Alpha-Spirit*.

Learning to observe the patterns in ourselves and others helps us manage everyday life better. It assists us in understanding "why" we are *feeling* the way we do. It also shines light on "why" another individual is *communicating* the way they are—and even what *behavior* we might expect from them as a result.

Our goal in *Systemology* is to reach a level of *Self-Honesty* that allows us to rise above restrictive viewpoints of *Beta-Existence*, to realize just how much "*more than Human*" we really are, and to know with utmost certainty that there are much "higher" *Universes*—only forgotten—for us to *return* to *again* as *Alpha-Spirits*.

PRACTICE EXERCISES

1. Can you recall a pleasant moment? What happened? How long ago was it? Where did it take place? Who was there? What did you like about it? You may have heard the expression: "think a happy thought." At times when a person is feeling emotional turbulence or stressed, the quickest remedy is to *locate* a pleasant incident and *notice* something about it. When an individual becomes overwhelmed or confused, it is generally helpful to go back and work from a point of certainty or "stable knowingness." Should you find any such difficulties with *Systemology* studies or exercises (or elsewhere in everyday

life), simply apply the suggestions from this first practice.

2. Look around the room. Locate an object. Notice something about it. Do this with several objects. Notice many things about the same object. Identify only what you can actually *see* about these objects. Make no assumptions, computations or considerations otherwise. Continue this practice until the room seems "brighter." Many individuals associate the concept of *"Awareness"* (or "being aware") with the idea of someone "knowing" (with certainty) what is going on around them and being "observant." This is quite accurate. The ability to "observe clearly" is a practiced skill. Only by confronting existence *"As-It-Is"* will we have our full power of *Awareness* to affect it.

3. Consider some individuals who are (or have been) influential in your life. With each one, *spot* them on the *Beta-Awareness Scale* —which is to say, *locate* the position on the scale that they seem (or seemed) to be operating from consistently. What did you *notice* (or *recall*) about the individual that resulted in your decision? How are you similar to this person? How are you different? Oftentimes, we will take on characteristics and personality traits of those closest to us—especially those we admire or consider an "ally" to our continued survival. It even happens out of "sympathy" for those we have lost. An individual may adjust their own "tone" or "energy" to be in better communication with a person operating at a certain

Awareness level—so long as they are *knowingly* doing so. *Fragment-ation* allows the "basic personality" of the *Alpha-Spirit* to be affected *unknowingly*.

4. Go to a public place where you can directly observe other people performing activities and/or interacting. Practice your "observation" skills and understanding of the *Beta-Awareness Scale*. When you *observe* an individual, *notice* things about them—facial expressions, body position, &tc.—and *spot* them on the scale with your best estimation. [Keep this evaluation to yourself.] If your situation allows for you to continue observing afterward, see if any further communications or behaviors prompt you to change your opinion. Practice observing different individuals this way.

5. Locate a "neutral" object—one that you do not have strong feelings of *liking* or *dislike* toward. Get the sense of feeling *indifferent* about it—actually deciding or *intending* to be *indifferent* toward it. Decide to now be suddenly very *interested* in it—and get the sense of actually being *interested* in it. Now, decide to be *afraid* of it—and get the sense of really feeling that. Choose various positions on the *Beta-Awareness Scale* for practicing this. End off on the same "neutral" state you started with. An *Alpha-Spirit* may certainly decide to *knowingly* experience an entire range of potential sensations, feelings or emotions. But, *fragmentation* causes these reactive-responses without *Self-Determination*.

6. Locate a "neutral" object—as with the previous exercise. This time, get the sense of *intending* for the *object* itself to genuinely "feel" the various positions on the *Beta-Awareness Scale*, from its viewpoint. Each time, get the idea that the object is "feeling" this reaction toward you—so, *afraid* of you, or *interested* in you, or *angry* at you, *&tc*. Does confronting any of these states change the way you feel? Do you make your intentions as a "silent command"? Or, does a certain *"image"* come to mind for each state? Maintaining one's own "inner composure" is the key to remaining at "cause" while confronting the nature of *Reality "As-It-Is."* The less we are reacting "on automatic," the more *Actualized Awareness* we can apply to managing our own *Self-Determined* existence.

7. The final exercise of the first lesson is to apply an understanding of the *Beta-Awareness Scale* and *observe* your *Self*. Have you spotted your own chronic state on the scale? Keep in mind—we do not mean how things are when watching your favorite movie, or getting a visit from an unwelcome guest. We are interested in the underlying continuous position from which we view the world. In addition to this, we *do* want to observe the fluctuations —and take notice of the circumstances that surround this. We also want to make records of these changes; how far they shift and for how long.

Continue learning
The Fundamentals of Systemology
in your next
Basic Course
lesson booklet:

REALITIES IN AGREEMENT:
SPIRITUAL LIFE AND THE UNIVERSE

GLOSSARY

actualization : to make actual, not just potential; to bring into full solid Reality; to realize fully in *Awareness* as a "thing."

agreement (reality) : unanimity of opinion of what is "thought" to be known; an accepted arrangement of how things are; things we consider as "real" or as an "is" of "reality"; a consensus of what is real as made by standard-issue (common) participants; what an individual contributes to or accepts as "real"; in *Systemology*, a synonym for "*reality.*"

alpha : the first, primary, basic, superior or beginning of some form; in *Systemology*, referring to the state of existence operating on spiritual archetypes and postulates, will and intention "exterior" to the low-level condensation and solidarity of energy and matter as the 'physical universe'.

alpha-spirit : a "spiritual" *Life*-form; the "true" *Self* or I-AM; the *individual*; the spiritual (*alpha*) *Self* that is animating the (*beta*) physical body or "*genetic vehicle*" using a continuous *Lifeline* of spiritual ("*ZU*") energy; an individual spiritual (*alpha*) entity possessing no physical mass or measurable waveform (motion) in the Physical Universe as itself, so it animates the (*beta*) physical body or "*genetic vehicle*" as a catalyst to experience *Self*-determined causality in effect within the *Physical Universe*; a singular unit or point of *Spiritual Awareness* that is *Aware* that it is *Aware.*

alpha thought : the highest spiritual *Self-determination* over creation and existence exercised by an Alpha-Spirit; the Alpha range of pure *Creative Ability* based on direct postulates and considerations of *Beingness*; spiritual qualities comparable to "thought" but originating in Alpha-existence (at "6.0") independently superior to a *beta-anchored* Mind-System, although an Alpha-Spirit may use Will ("5.0") to carry the intentions of a postulate or consideration ("6.0") to the Master Control Center ("4.0").

ascension : actualized *Awareness* elevated to the point of true "spiritual existence" exterior to *beta existence*. An "Ascended Master" is one who has returned to an incarnation on Earth as an inherently *Enlightened One*, demonstrable in their actions—they have the ability to *Self-direct* the "Spirit" as *Self* and maintain consciousness beyond this existence as a personal identity continuum with the same *Self-directed* control and communication of Will-Intention that is exercised, actualized and developed deliberately during one's present incarnation.

attention : active use of *Awareness* toward a specific aspect or thing; the act of "attending" with the presence of *Self*; a direction of focus or concentration of *Awareness* along a particular channel or conduit or toward a particular terminal node or communication termination point; the Self-directed concentration of personal energy as a combination of observation, thought-waves and consideration; focused application of *Self-Directed Awareness*.

awareness : the highest sense of-and-as Self in knowing and being as I-AM (the *Alpha-Spirit*); the extent of beingness directed as a POV experienced by Self as knowingness.

beta (awareness) : all consciousness activity ("*Awareness*") in the "Physical Universe" (KI) or else *beta-existence*; *Awareness* within the range of the *genetic-body*, including material thoughts, emotional responses and physical motors; personal *Awareness* of physical energy and physical matter moving through physical space and experienced as "time"; the *Awareness* held by *Self* that is restricted to a physical organic

Lifeform or "*genetic vehicle*" in which it experiences causality in the *Physical Universe*.

beta (existence) : all manifestation in the "Physical Universe" (KI); the "Physical" state of existence consisting of vibrations of physical energy and physical matter moving through physical space and experienced as "time"; the conditions of *Awareness* for the *Alpha-spirit* (*Self*) as a physical organic *Lifeform* or "*genetic vehicle*" in which it experiences causality in the *Physical Universe*.

beta-defragmentation : toward a state of *Self-Honesty* in regards to handling experience of the "Physical Universe" (*beta-existence*); an applied spiritual philosophy (or technology) of Self-Actualization

consideration : careful analytical reflection of all aspects; deliberation; determining the significance of a "thing" in relation to similarity or dissimilarity to other "things"; evaluation of facts and importance of certain facts; thorough examination of all aspects related to, or important for, making a decision; the analysis of consequences and estimation of significance when making decisions.

defragmentation : the *reparation* of wholeness; collecting all dispersed parts to reform an original whole; a process of removing "*fragmenta-tion*" in data or knowledge to provide a clear understanding; applying techniques and processes that promote a *holistic* interconnected *alpha* state, favoring observational *Awareness* of continuity in all spiritual and physical systems; in *Systemology*, a "*Seeker*" achieving an actualized state of basic "*Self-Honest Awareness*" is said to have completed *beta-defragmentation*, whereas *Alpha-defragmentation* is the rehabilitation of the *creative ability*, managing the *Spiritual Timeline* and the POV of *Self* as Alpha-Spirit (I-AM).

existence : the *state* or fact of *apparent manifestation*; the resulting combination of the Principles of Manifestation: consciousness, motion and substance; continued *survival*; that which independently exists.

exterior : outside of; on the outside; in *Systemology*, we mean specifically the POV of *Self* that is '*outside of*' the *Human Condition,* free of the physical and mental trappings of the Physical Universe; a metahuman range of consideration; see also '*Zu-Vision*'.

external : a force coming from outside; information received from outside sources; in *Systemology*, the objective '*Physical Universe*' existence, or *beta-existence*, that the Physical

Body or *genetic vehicle* is essentially *anchored* to for its considerations of locational space-time as a dimension or POV.

facets : an aspect, an apparent phase; one of many faces of something; a cut surface on a gem or crystal; in *Systemology*—a single perception or aspect of a memory or "*Imprint*"; any one of many ways in which a memory is recorded; perceptions associated with a painful emotional (sensation) experience and "*imprinted*" onto a metaphoric lens through which to view future similar experiences; other secondary terminals that are associated with a particular terminal, painful event or experience of loss, and which may exhibit the same encoded significance as the activating event.

fragmentation : breaking into parts and scattering the pieces; the *fractioning* of wholeness or the *fracture* of a holistic interconnected *alpha* state, favoring observational *Awareness* of perceived connectivity between parts; *discontinuity*; separation of a totality into parts; in *Systemology*, a person outside a state of *Self-Honesty* is said to be *fragmented*.

genetic-vehicle : a physical *Life*-form; the physical (*beta*) body that is animated/controlled by the (*Alpha*) *Spirit* using a continuous *Lifeline* (ZU); a physical (*beta*) organic receptacle and catalyst for the (*Alpha*) *Self* to operate "causes" and experience "effects" within the *Physical Universe*.

gradient : a degree of partitioned ascent or descent along some scale, elevation or incline; "higher" and "lower" values in relation to one another.

holistic : the examination of interconnected systems as encompassing something greater than the *sum* of their "parts."

interior : inside of; on the inside; in *Systemology*, we mean specifically the POV of *Self* that is fixed to the *'internal'* *Human Condition,* including the *Reactive Control Center* (RCC) and Mind-System or *Master Control Center* (MCC); within *beta-existence*.

internal : a force coming from inside; information received from inside sources; in *Systemology*, the objective experience of *beta-existence* that is associated with the Physical Body or *genetic vehicle* and its POV regarding sensation and perception; from inside the body; within the body.

Human Condition : a standard default state of Human experience, generally accepted to be the extent of its potential identity (*beingness*).

imprint : to strongly impress, stamp, mark (or

outline) onto a softer 'impressible' substance; to mark with pressure onto a surface; in *Systemology*, used to indicate permanent Reality impressions marked by frequencies, energies or interactions experienced during periods of emotional distress, pain, unconsciousness, loss, enforcement, or something antagonistic to physical (personal) survival, all of which are are stored with other reactive response-mechanisms at lower-levels of *Awareness* as opposed to the active memory database and proactive processing center of the Mind; an experiential "memory-set" that may later resurface—be triggered or stimulated artificially—as Reality, of which similar responses will be engaged automatically; holographic-like imagery "stamped" onto consciousness as composed of energetic *facets* tied to the "snap-shot" of an experience.

knowledge : clear personal processing of informed understanding; information (data) that is actualized as effectively workable understanding; a demonstrable understanding on which we may 'set' our *Awareness*—or literally a "knowledge."

Master-Control-Center (MCC) : a perfect computing device to the extent of the information received from "lower levels" of sensory experience/perception; the proactive communication system of the "*Mind*"; a relay point of active *Awareness* along the Identity's *ZU-line*, which is responsible for maintaining basic *Self-Honest Clarity* of *Knowingness* as a *seat of consciousness* between the *Alpha-Spirit* and the secondary "*Reactive Control Center*" of a *Life-form* in *beta existence*; the Mind-center for an *Alpha-Spirit* to actualize cause in the *beta existence*; the analytical *Self-Determined* Mind-center of an *Alpha-Spirit used* to project *Will* toward the genetic body; the point of contact between *Spiritual Systems* and the *beta existence*; presumably the "*Third Eye*" of a being connected directly to the *I-AM-Self*, which is responsible for *determining* Reality at any time; in *Systemology*, this is plotted at (4.0) on the continuity model of the *ZU-line*.

mental image : a subjectively experienced "picture" created and imagined into being by the Alpha-Spirit (or at lower levels, one of its automated mechanisms) that includes all perceptible *facets* of totally immersive scene, which may be forms originated by an individual, or a "facsimile-copy" ("snap-shot") of something seen or encountered; a duplication of wave-forms in one's Personal Universe as a "picture" that mirror an "external" Universe experience, such as an *Imprint*.

point-of-view (POV) : a point to view from; an opinion or attitude as expressed from a specific identity-phase; a specific standpoint or vantage-point; a definitive manner of consideration specific to an individual phase or identity; a place or position affording a specific view or vantage; circumstances and programming of an individual that is conducive to a particular response, consideration or belief-set (paradigm); a position (consideration) or place (location) that provides a specific view or perspective (subjective) on experience (of the objective). May also be referred to in our texts as a "*viewpoint.*"

processing, systematic : the inner-workings or "through-put" result of systems; in *Systemology*, a methodology of applied spiritual technology used toward personal Self-Actualization; methods of selective directed attention, communicated language and associative imagery that targets an increase in personal control of the human condition.

reactive control center (RCC) : the secondary (reactive) communication system of the "*Mind*"; a relay point of *Awareness* along the Identity's *ZU-line*, which is responsible for engaging basic motors, biochemical processes and any *programmed automated responses* of a living *beta* organism; the reactive Mind-Center of

89

a living organism relaying communications of *Awareness* between causal experience of *Physical Systems* and the "*Master Control Center*"; it presumably stores all emotional encoded imprints as fragmentation of "chakra" frequencies of *ZU* (within the range of the "*psychological/emotive systems*" of a being), which it may *react* to as Reality at any time; in *Systemology*, this is plotted at (2.0) on the continuity model of the *ZU-line*.

reality : see "*agreement.*"

Seeker : an individual on the *Pathway to Self-Honesty*; a practitioner of *Mardukite Systemology* or *Systemology Processing* that is working toward *Spiritual Ascension*.

Self-actualization : bringing the full potential of the Human spirit into Reality; expressing full capabilities and creativeness of the *Alpha-Spirit*.

Self-determinism : the freedom to act, clear of external control or influence; the personal control of Will to direct intention.

Self-honesty : the basic or original *alpha* state of *being* and *knowing*; clear and present total *Awareness* of-and-as *Self*, in its most basic and true proactive expression of itself as *Spirit* or *I-AM*—free of artificial attachments, perceptive filters and other emotionally-reactive or mentally-conditioned programming imposed on the human condition by the systematized physical world; the ability to experience existence without judgment.

Standard Model, The (systemology) : our existential and cosmological *standard model* or cabbalistic model; a "*monistic continuity model*" demonstrating *total system* interconnectivity "above" and "below" observation of any apparent *parameters*; the original presentation of the *ZU-line*, represented as a singular vertical (*y*-axis) waveform in space across dimensional levels or Universes (*Spheres of Existence*) without charting any specific movement across a dimensional time-graph *x*-axis; The Standard Model of Systemology represents the basic workable synthesis of common denominators in models explored throughout Grade-I and Grade-II material.

system : from the Greek, "to set together"; to set or arrange things or data together so as to form an orderly understanding of a "whole."

thought-form : apparent *manifestation* or existential *realization* of *Thought-waves* as "solids" even when only apparent in Reality-agreements of the Observer; the treatment of *Thought-waves* as permanent *imprints* obscuring *Self-Honest* clarity of *Awareness* when reinforced

91

by emotional experience as actualized "thought-formed solids" ("*beliefs*") in the Mind; energetic patterns that "surround" the individual.

ZU : the ancient Sumerian cuneiform sign for the archaic verb—"*to know*," "*knowingness*" or "*awareness*"; in *Mardukite Zuism and Systemology*, the active energy/matter of the "Spiritual Universe" (AN) experienced as a *Lifeforce* or *consciousness* that imbues living forms extant in the "Physical Universe" (KI); "*Spiritual Life Energy*"; energy demonstrated by the WILL of an actualized *Alpha-Spirit* in the "Spiritual Universe" (AN), which impinges its *Awareness* into the Physical Universe (KI), animating/controlling *Life* for its experience of *beta-existence* along an individual Alpha-Spirit's personal *Identity-continuum*, called a *ZU-line*.

Zu-Line : a theoretical construct in *Mardukite Zuism and Systemology* demonstrating *Spiritual Life Energy* (ZU) as a personal individual "continuum" of Awareness interacting with all Spheres of Existence on the Standard Model of Systemology; a spectrum of potential variations and interactions of a monistic continuum or singular *Spiritual Life Energy (ZU)* demonstrated on the Standard Model; an energetic channel of potential POV and "locations" of Beingness, demonstrated in early Systemology materials as

92

an individual Alpha-Spirit's personal *Identity-continuum*, potentially connecting *Awareness (ZU)* of *Self* with "*Infinity*" simultaneous with all points considered in existence; a symbolic demonstration of the "*Life-line*" on which *Awareness (ZU)* extends from the direction of the "Spiritual Universe" (AN) in its true original *alpha state* through an entire possible range of activity resulting in its *beta state* and control of a *genetic-entity* occupying the *Physical Universe (KI)*.

Zu-Vision : the true and basic (*Alpha*) Point-of-View (perspective, POV) maintained by *Self* as *Alpha-Spirit* outside boundaries or considerations of the *Human Condition* "Mind-Systems" and *exterior* to beta-existence reality agreements with the Physical Universe; a POV of Self *as* "a unit of Spiritual Awareness" that exists independent of a "body" and entrapment in a *Human Condition*; "spirit vision" in its truest sense.

THE SYSTEMOL

Seekers and students of the *Basic Course* and *Professional Course* will also be interested in the *Advanced Series* of the *Systemology Core*. These volumes are a complete chronological record of the Mardukite New Thought developments from the Systemology Society, published in 2019 through 2023.

The *Systemology Core* begins with the first professional publication released when the *Mardukite Systemology Society* emerged from the underground in 2019, with: *"The Tablets of Destiny Revelation."*

OGY PATHWAY

The Tablets of Destiny Revelation:
*How Long-Lost Anunnaki Wisdom
Can Change the Fate of Humanity*

Crystal Clear: *Handbook for Seekers*

Metahuman Destinations (*2 volumes*)

Imaginomicon:
Approaching Gateways to Higher Universes

Way of the Wizard: *Utilitarian Systemology*

Systemology-180: *Fast-Track to Ascension*

Systemology Backtrack:
Reclaiming Spiritual Power & Past-Life Memory

PUBLISHED BY THE **JOSHUA FREE** IMPRINT REPRESENTING

The Mardukite Academy of Systemology

THE JOSHUA FREE IMPRINT
JFI PUBLICATIONS

MARDUKITE
ZUISM

mardukite.com

www.ingramcontent.com/pod-product-compliance
Lightning Source LLC
Chambersburg PA
CBHW071211120626
46546CB00006B/2510